AVOCA
Tea Time

Contents

Introduction

aking evokes feelings of warmth and contentment: a cake in the oven, shortbread cooling on a wire rack, biscuits being stacked for later consumption. In a world as fast-moving as ours, baking is a perfect antidote. It is generous and uplifting and can be nostalgic or creative.

Many Avoca customers tell us they would love to bake but have neither the skill, equipment nor time. This book is about challenging those three obstacles. With no more than a wooden spoon and a bowl you can start with the muffins on page 10. These are so simple a child could make them. Indeed this is one of the fun aspects of baking: children adore it and are often surprisingly good. Jam tarts, for instance, look stunning and really are easy.

If you think baking is an exact science, try the cobbler on page 36. Sure, attention to detail in the measuring of ingredients is required, but this is a gloriously rustic tart that epitomises the idea of something home made. And if you have aspirations for proper high tea, try the ultimate chocolate cake on page 38. This is really easy to make, doesn't even require a mixer and is fool-proof.

Baking is an area of cooking that cries out for tips and this book is full of them. Here we share in-house knowledge to help you on the way. The single most important tip is to get to know your oven. All have their own quirks and personalities and these need exploring.

Part of baking's attraction is its purity. Simple, honest ingredients. Which is not what you get when you buy something made in a factory.

Quantities are indicated for each recipe where appropriate.

Lemon drizzle cake

225g unsalted butter
225g caster sugar
4 medium-sized eggs, beaten
225g self-raising flour
½ teaspoon baking powder
35g ground almonds
juice of 1 lemon or 2 limes
finely grated zest of 1 lemon
or 2 limes
225g mixed berries

Drizzle topping
finely grated zest and juice
of 3 lemons
175g caster sugar

This is a simple, old-fashioned cake. Its zesty, lemon tang complements the sponge and the pile of fruit on top. A perfect summer cake and just the thing for tea in the garden.

Preheat the oven to 150C/gas mark 2. Lightly grease a 23cm springform tin, and then line with baking parchment.

Cream the butter and sugar together until pale and fluffy. Gradually add the eggs, then fold in the flour, baking powder and ground almonds. Fold in the zest and juice of the lemons and half the fruit. Place the mix in the tin and top with the remaining fruit. Bake for an hour then remove from the tin and transfer to a wire rack.

Combine the lemon juice and zest for the topping with the sugar in a small saucepan. Heat to dissolve the sugar then pour over the cake while it is still warm so that it seeps in.

When the cake has cooled, top with extra fruit and serve.

Festive fruit cake

Makes 1 round cake

*325g each of sultanas,
currants and raisins
150g glace cherries
75g mixed peel, chopped
finely grated zest of 1 orange
and 1 lemon
100ml Irish whiskey, plus a
little extra
2 cooking apples
75g nibbed almonds
275g unsalted butter
275g light brown sugar
7 medium-sized eggs
350g plain flour
75g ground almonds*

Best made some weeks ahead of intended consumption. This is one cake that needs time so all the ingredients get to know each other. As the cake ages the flavours will mellow out and become more complex.

Wash all the dried fruit and place in a large bowl along with the orange and lemon zest. Pour over the whiskey and leave overnight.

Preheat the oven to 150C/gas mark 2. Have ready a 23cm round cake tin, greased and lined with parchment.

Peel and grate the cooking apples, and add to the fruit along with the nibbed almonds.

In a mixer, cream the butter, sugar and eggs together, then gradually add in the flour. Finally fold in the ground almonds, the fruit and nuts, then pour into the prepared tin.

Wrap brown paper round the outside of the tin so it stands at least 5cm higher than the top of the tin - this is to prevent the edges burning.

Bake for 40 minutes, then reduce the oven temperature to 120C/gas mark ½ and bake for another 40 minutes or until a skewer inserted comes out clean.

When just out of the oven pour over the remaining whiskey, then leave to cool in the tin.

Low GI pumpkin bread

Makes 1 loaf

250g coarse wholewheat
flour
250g spelt flour
2 tablespoons pumpkin seeds
1 level teaspoon bread soda,
sieved
1 teaspoon salt
1 teaspoon caster sugar
(optional)
approx. 400ml buttermilk

GI stands for 'glycaemic index'. This measures the speed at which foods are broken down by the body to form glucose, the body's source of energy. High GI foods break down quickly and leave you feeling hungry. Low GI foods, like whole grains and dried fruit break down more slowly and leave you feeling fuller for longer. It is these low GI foods that form the core of the diet.

Preheat the oven to 170C/gas mark 3. Grease a 900g loaf tin.
    Combine the dry ingredients, stir in the buttermilk and mix together. Spoon into the loaf tin and bake for 50 minutes to an hour.
    Remove from the oven and tin, and transfer to a wire rack to cool.

Variations

You could add 2 tablespoons of any seeds – sunflower, linseed or hemp are particularly good – or a mixture to the bread, or dried fruit, like diced apricots, cranberries or sultanas.

Tip

We use Ballybrado organic flour. Experiment to find a flour that works for you. They are all very different.

Muffins

**Makes 15 large or
30 small muffins**

450g self-raising flour
225g caster sugar
1 level teaspoon baking
powder
225ml milk
225g unsalted butter
2 medium-sized eggs, beaten

Some of the easiest baking in this book. Muffins require no equipment and don't take very long to make or bake. You can also bake the mixture below as a loaf or cake, in which case cook for 50 minutes. Perfect for school fêtes.

Preheat the oven to 180C/gas mark 4 and have 15 muffin tins ready.

Mix the flour, caster sugar and baking powder together in a large bowl and make a well in the centre. Heat the milk and butter together until the butter melts. Allow to cool, then add to the dry mixture with the eggs.

Spoon into the muffin cases and bake for 20 minutes (6-8 minutes if you are doing mini ones).

Additions

You can add the following to the mixture to ring the changes.

200g raspberries and 1 nectarine, chopped.
1 pear, trimmed and diced
1 tablespoon each of chocolate buttons and slivered almonds
Triple chocolate: 1 tablespoon each of white, milk and dark chocolate buttons

Baking Tips

Baking has an image of old-fashioned existence where there is endless time and little pressure. Something far from our busy modern lives. In reality a lot of baking is very quick and most of what time it does take is oven time.

The Baker's Storecupboard

Having most of the ingredients in your storecupboard, fruit bowl and fridge is half the battle. The following is what a good baker would have available. But be aware that nothing lasts for ever. Flour may look pretty inert, but it doesn't go on indefinitely.

Almonds

Baking powder

Bicarbonate of soda

Buttermilk

Digestive biscuits

Dried fruit, eg figs,
    sultanas, raisins

Full-fat milk

Golden caster sugar

Good quality unsalted
    butter

Good quality strawberry
    jam

Good quality chocolate

Good quality cocoa

Lemons

Light brown sugar

Natural almond extract

Nuts, eg pecans, walnuts,
    whole almonds (grind
    as you use them for a
    better flavour)

Organic eggs

Organic flours

Porridge oats

Seeds, eg pumpkin,
sunflower, poppy and
    sesame

Soft dark brown sugar

Vanilla extract, not essence

Measurements

Measurements are more exact than in any other branch of cooking but too often this is taken literally. You need to feel your ingredients. There is no point in adding all the milk if the mixture ends up being sloppy. Be patient and explore.

There are many who say pastry cooks are born, that it is impossible to learn baking. This has not been our experience. Baking is no different from any other area of cooking. Working with ingredients, seeing how they react with each other, experimenting – all this is as valid with baking as it is with any other cooking.

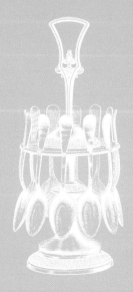

Rocky road biscuits

Makes 12-15

480g milk chocolate, broken
into pieces
100g digestive biscuits
80g marshmallows,
cut in half
80g shelled hazelnuts,
skinned and toasted

These biscuits are really easy to make and perfect if you've children keen on doing a little baking.

Place the chocolate in a bowl over a saucepan of barely simmering water. Melt gently, stirring occasionally.

Line a lightly greased Swiss roll tin with baking parchment. Roughly break up the biscuits by hand and put in the bottom of the tin. Dot half the marshmallows and all of the hazelnuts around the biscuits. Pour the melted chocolate over the top, and shake the tin to get an even mix. Dot with the remaining marshmallows over the top.

Chill in the fridge until just set. Remove and cut into squares using a sharp knife.

Strawberry meringue roulade

4 large egg whites
225g caster sugar
300ml double cream,
whipped
450g strawberries, sliced
or quartered
Extra whipped cream and
strawberries, to decorate

This is a favourite in Avoca. It combines sticky meringue with the best of summer fruit ... And lots of cream! What could be a better way to finish a summer lunch outside?

Line a 30 x 20cm swiss roll tin with baking parchment. Put the egg whites and half the caster sugar into a bowl and use an electric whisk to whisk to snowy peaks. Then gradually add the remaining sugar, continuing to whisk for 10–15 minutes, until it forms stiff peaks.

Spread the mixture into the tin and bake for 1 hour in an oven preheated to 150C/gas mark 2. Remove from the oven and cool. Turn out on to a fresh sheet of baking parchment and carefully peel off the lining paper. Spread over the cream and strawberries and roll up.

Chocolate meringue roulade

5 eggs, separated
175g caster sugar
175g dark chocolate
(55 per cent cocoa solids)
75ml water
300ml double cream
Icing sugar and chocolate
wafers, to decorate
Serves 8–10

Line a 28 x 35cm swiss roll tin with foil and grease lightly. Whisk the egg yolks and caster sugar together until the mixture is pale and mousselike and holds a figure of eight when trailed from the whisk. This needs to be done with an electric beater as it is virtually impossible to do by hand.

Put the chocolate and water in a bowl set over a pan of simmering water and leave until the chocolate has melted, stirring occasionally until smooth. Leave to cool slightly and then fold into the egg yolk mixture.

Whisk the egg whites until they form stiff peaks, then fold them into the chocolate mixture.

Pour into the tin and bake in an oven preheated to 180C/gas mark 4 for 12–15 minutes, until firm to the touch in the centre.

Remove from the oven, cover with a damp tea towel and leave to cool. Turn the roulade out on to a sheet of baking parchment and peel off the foil.

Whip the cream and spread it evenly on top, then roll up, using the baking parchment to help. Dust with icing sugar and garnish with chocolate wafers.

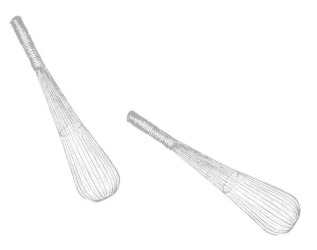

Key Lime Pie

Base

225g ginger-nut biscuits, crushed
95g unsalted butter, melted and cooled

Filling

3 large egg yolks
finely grated zest of 3 limes
400g condensed milk
150ml lime juice (about 4-5 large limes)

To decorate

crème fraîche

So-called because the limes traditionally used to make it came from the Florida Keys. These limes are said to be more tart and aromatic than the more common Persian limes but the pie is delicious when made with either.

Preheat the oven to 180C/gas mark 4. Line a loose-bottomed 23cm flan tin, 2.5cm deep, with baking parchment.

Mix the crushed ginger-nut biscuits with the cooled melted butter. Press firmly into the base and sides of the tin. Bake for 10-12 minutes until crisp and golden.

For the filling, place the egg yolks and zest in a bowl and whisk with an electric mixer for about 4 minutes, or until the egg has thickened. Add the condensed milk and whisk for a further 4 minutes. Finally add the lime juice and whisk for a minute to incorporate. Pour over the baked crust and return to the oven for a further 20 minutes.

Remove from the oven and, when cold, cover and chill until required. Decorate with crème fraîche.

Carrot cake

400g caster sugar
4 eggs
400ml sunflower oil
400g self-raising flour
1 teaspoon mixed spice
1 teaspoon salt
400g carrots, grated
1 teaspoon vanilla extract

For the topping
175g full-fat cream
cheese
50g unsalted butter
Juice and grated zest of
½ lemon
350g icing sugar

Makes 2 loaves

This recipe comes from Jill, one of the first people to bake cakes for the fledgling café at Kilmacanogue. All attempts to better it have failed, so we pass the recipe on unchanged, all the nicer for having stood the test of time.

Line two 900g loaf tins with baking parchment. Whisk the sugar, eggs and oil together until thick and pale, then mix in the flour, mixed spice and salt. This is best done in an electric mixer with the balloon whisk. Stir in the carrots and vanilla essence.

Pour the mixture into the loaf tins and bake in an oven preheated to 170C/gas mark 3 for 1 hour or until a skewer inserted in the centre comes out clean. Leave to cool in the tins for 10 minutes, then turn out on to a wire rack to cool completely.

To make the topping, beat the cream cheese, butter, lemon juice and zest together, then beat in the icing sugar. Spread on top of the cooled cakes.

Chocolate Raspberry Cheesecake Brownies

Makes 16 squares

Brownie base
*200g dark chocolate (70%
cocoa solids), broken into
pieces*
200g unsalted butter
250g caster sugar
4 medium-sized eggs, beaten
110g plain flour

Cheesecake topping
400g cream cheese
150g caster sugar
2 medium-sized eggs, beaten
1 drop vanilla extract
120g raspberries

The best of both the brownie and cheesecake worlds, and worth every mouthful.

Preheat the oven to 150C/gas mark 2. Line a 22 x 22 x 8cm tin with baking parchment.

For the brownie base, melt the chocolate in a bowl set in a saucepan of barely simmering water. Remove and allow to cool slightly.

Cream the butter and sugar together until pale and thickened. Add the eggs gradually, then add the flour, and finally stir in the melted chocolate. Spread the mixture out evenly in the tin.

For the topping, whisk the cream cheese and sugar together, then mix in the eggs and vanilla. Spoon this mixture on top of the brownie mixture and scatter over the raspberries.

Bake for 45 minutes until almost set but still slightly wobbly. Allow to cool before cutting into squares.

Tips

To cut, place the knife in a jug of boiling water and wipe clean between each cut to get a clean slice. You need to work fast so the knife stays hot. Use a palette knife or fish slice to remove from the tin. Store in an airtight container in the fridge. Eat within 4 days.

Equipment

Baking equipment is inexpensive to buy. However rather than go out and get everything immediately it is far better to build up slowly, that way your equipment will more closely reflect the kind of baking you do.

A mixer makes things a lot easier. You need a balloon whisk when you need to get air into something: sponges and meringues, for example. The K beater is more for mixing ingredients, like fairy buns and brownies, for example.

Ovens

As mentioned above, ovens vary widely. By this we mean the actual temperature may vary from the stated temperature on the dial. They also often have hot spots so something to the right is more likely to burn than if it is on the left. You need to get to know your oven so you can work with these variations.

Preheating is vital. It should be the first thing you do.

Baking times can also be an issue. As a rule, start to check things as you come into the last quarter of the cooking time. It's better to catch or twist something to get an even colouring than end up with something golden brown on one side and raw on the other.

Uneven numbers

This is a simple rule which works, although nobody seems quite sure why. Uneven numbers look better than even ones, so decorate in 3, 5, 7 or 9.

Baking parchment

This is much better to use than greaseproof paper. It is more substantial.

Apricot jam

When heated and poured through a sieve, it makes a very professional glaze. Brush on top of tarts for a shiny finish.

Vanilla and almond

Place used vanilla pods in Kilner jars with caster sugar. The vanilla flavour transfers over time.

Only use natural vanilla and almond extract, some of the more commercial ones are scary. If you cannot get natural, then better to leave it out altogether.

Sieving

Sieving is a good idea when baking. It helps to keep things light and airy. Always sieve your bread soda and cake and pastry flour and icing sugar when it goes into pastry.

Folding

When a recipe says to 'fold' something in, it means try to keep what air is in the mixture intact. This is done by using the sharp side of a preferably metal spoon. Cut into the centre of the mixture and fold over gently. Turn the bowl and repeat until everything is incorporated.

Lemon tart with caramelised strawberries

1 quantity of shortcrust
pastry (see page 55)
400g caster sugar
Juice of 5 lemons
Grated zest of 3 lemons
8 eggs
350ml double cream,
whipped
Icing sugar for dusting

**For the caramelised
strawberries**
225g caster sugar
4 tablespoons water
8 large strawberries

*This is Fleur Campbell's recipe for a really classic tart. It has
real zest, a perfect way to end a meal or pep you up in the
afternoon.*

Roll out the pastry, use to line a 28cm x 4cm deep fluted
tart tin and bake blind (see page 55). Put the sugar and
lemon juice in a large bowl and stir until the sugar has
dissolved. Add the lemon zest, sieve and then whisk in the
eggs and finally stir in the cream. For best results, leave the
filling overnight in the fridge, then remove and stir gently to
combine it again. If you don't leave it overnight it will
separate during cooking, giving a custard bottom and foamy
top. Pour the filling into the baked pastry case and cook in
a preheated oven 140C/gas mark 1 for 1 hour, until set.
Remove from the oven and leave to cool.

To make the caramel, put the sugar and water in a
saucepan and heat gently until the sugar has dissolved.
Increase the heat and boil until it has changed colour to a
light caramel. Dip the strawberries in one at a time, holding
them on a fork, and place on an oiled baking sheet to cool.
To serve, dust the tart thickly with icing sugar and then
caramelise it, if liked, under a very hot grill or with a cook's
blowtorch. Decorate with the caramelised strawberries.

Multi-seed flapjacks

Makes about 20

450g porridge oats
110g light brown sugar
150g sultanas
150g dried apricots, diced
150g mixed seeds (pumpkin,
sunflower and sesame)
275g unsalted butter
200g honey

These are sweet from the fruit but packed with seeds which give them a healthy edge. Perfect for a lunchbox or picnic treat.

Preheat the oven to 150C/gas mark 2. Grease and line a 33 x 23cm Swiss roll tin with parchment paper.

Place all the dry ingredients in a bowl. Melt the butter with the honey over a low heat and pour into the dry mixture. Stir well to incorporate.

Spoon the mixture into the lined tin and bake for 25-30 minutes or until golden brown.

Allow to cool slightly, then cut into squares while still warm. Transfer to a wire rack to cool.

Cheese and sun-dried tomato scones

450g flour
1 teaspoon of baking powder
generous pinch salt
1/4 teaspoon cayenne pepper
110g butter, cubed
50g grated mature cheddar
8 semi sun-dried tomatoes,
chopped
8 pitted black olives, roughly
chopped
200-300ml milk (you want a
reasonably dry mixture)
1 egg

These savoury scones are a great accompaniment to soup or with cheese and chutney.

Mix all the dry ingredients together in a bowl with a generous pinch of salt. Add the butter and using your fingertips lightly work until it resembles dry breadcrumbs. Then add the cheese, semi-sun-dried tomatoes and olives. Add the egg and enough milk to moisten. Mix well until the mixture is a soft doughy texture - but not too moist. Gather into a ball and turn on to a floured surface. Roll lightly to a 3cm thickness with a rolling pin. Cut out and bake in a preheated oven, 180C/gas mark 4 for 12 to 15 minutes, or until well browned.

Traditional scones

Makes 12–18

450g self-raising flour
A pinch of baking powder
A generous pinch of salt
50g caster sugar
110g unsalted butter, diced
1 egg, lightly beaten
50ml double cream
200ml milk (you may need
a little more)
1 egg beaten with
1 tablespoon water, to glaze

Sift the flour, baking powder and salt into a bowl and stir in the sugar. Using your fingertips, lightly work in the butter until the mixture resembles dry breadcrumbs. Add the egg, cream and enough milk to moisten. Mix well until it has a soft, doughy texture – but it shouldn't be too moist. Gather the dough into a ball and turn it out on to a floured surface, then roll lightly with a rolling pin to 2.5cm thick. Cut out with a round cutter, transfer to a greased baking sheet and brush the tops with the egg glaze. Bake in an oven preheated to 180C/gas mark 4 for 15–20 minutes or until well browned.

Chocolate shortbread

Makes about 16

225g cold unsalted butter, diced
200g plain flour
110g cornflour
110g icing sugar
25g cocoa powder

You can dip this shortbread into melted milk chocolate and decorate as required, using jelly tots, or Smarties.

Preheat the oven to 110C/gas mark ¼.

Put all the ingredients into the bowl of a food mixer. Turn on very slowly with the beater and mix until everything comes together.

Roll out on a floured surface and cut with cutters (at Avoca we use heart and people shapes. Chill in the fridge for an hour.

Place on a parchment-lined baking sheet and bake for 1.5 hours. You need to allow 3cm around each biscuit so they can spread out. Allow to cool on wire racks. These will keep in an airtight container for 4-5 days.

Tips

If you don't rest the shortbread mixture in the fridge it won't hold its shape. You can hold the uncooked shortbread in the fridge until the next day

If you are storing shortbread, use baking parchment between each layer to keep them fresh.

Mixed berry
Normandy tart

*1 quantity of shortcrust
pastry (see page 55)
75g unsalted butter
75g caster sugar
1 egg and 1 egg yolk
A drop of natural almond
essence
65g ground almonds
40g plain flour, sifted
900g mixed berries, such as
strawberries, raspberries,
blackberries and blueberries
Apricot jam, to glaze
Serves 8–10*

Wonderfully versatile, this fruit and almond tart can be made with almost any soft fruit, allowing it to run throughout the summer depending on what is available. Good with cream, and excellent for breakfast the following morning if there is any left over.

Roll out the pastry and use to line a 23cm fluted flan tin. Beat the butter and sugar together until light and fluffy, then beat in the egg, egg yolk and almond essence. Fold in the ground almonds and flour. Spread this mixture inside the pastry case and sprinkle with 75–110g of the fruit. Bake in an oven preheated to 180C/gas mark 4 for 35 minutes, until lightly coloured and firm to the touch. Remove from the oven and leave to cool. Gently melt some apricot jam in a saucepan and then sieve it. Brush the sieved jam on top of the tart to glaze. Arrange the remaining fruit decoratively on top and then glaze again

Florentines

Makes 30 x 5cm florentines

150g unsalted butter
150g caster sugar
60g glacé cherries
100g flaked almonds
5 tablespoons double cream
50g mixed peel, chopped
50g sultanas
30g plain flour

To decorate
275g dark chocolate (53% cocoa solids), melted

These crispy chocolate thins are a teatime treat certainly, but also a great addition to a mid-morning shot of coffee, or to have with coffee after lunch or dinner.

Preheat the oven to 140C/gas mark 1. Line a couple of baking trays with baking parchment.

Heat the butter and sugar gently over a low heat in a saucepan until dissolved, then bring to the boil. Remove from the heat and add the remaining ingredients. Stir well until combined.

Place tablespoonfuls of the mixture on to the lined trays, spacing them well apart. Bake for 15-20 minutes, or until the edges are turning golden brown. Remove the tray from the oven and push the edges back into the centre. Return to the oven for 3-4 minutes or until golden brown all over. Remove and allow to cool on the trays for 10 minutes, then transfer to wire racks.

Decorate when cool with melted dark chocolate, either on one side as in the picture or dip in the chocolate so half the Florentine is covered in chocolate.

Weight watching

Calorie counters tend to avoid the whole idea of teatime, arguing it is one meal they can do without. The intention here is not to suggest you stop for tea every day. Rather than if and when you choose to do so, everything you eat can and should be made from scratch from the very best ingredients.

A little, occasionally, in tandem with exercise is something of a mantra with us. (When willpower allows!)

Shortcuts

All-butter frozen puff and shortcrust pastry. But it has to be all-butter, hydrogenated vegetable oil will not do.

Meringue shells bought from a good pastry shop.

A cool head

The success of baking is greatly assisted if the ingredients remain cool. This is why the pastry section in a restaurant kitchen is usually separate from the main stoves, and why people use marble surfaces. You too should be cool rather than flustered. Your ingredients need to know who is in charge!

Chilling

Pastry and cookie doughs need to rest in the fridge for at least an hour. If you skip this stage the dough will not hold its shape and will shrink when baking.

Icing sugar

Using icing sugar is a way to cover minor blips on many finished cakes and pastries. Pour some into a sieve and lightly tap above your chosen object. Rose petals are also useful in the summer.

Tea

Time

Jam tarts

Makes 10 x 9cm tarts or 36 tiny tarts

225g plain flour
150g unsalted butter, diced
25g icing sugar, sieved
2 medium-sized egg yolks
very good-quality jam
(raspberry, strawberry,
peach)

These are simple to make and quick to eat. If you use several different jams, you will have lots of colour as well.

Preheat the oven to 180C/gas mark 4. Rub the flour and butter together until the texture is like breadcrumbs, then stir in the icing sugar. Make a well in the centre. Add the egg yolks and just enough water to form a ball with the flour mixture. Wrap in clingfilm and leave to rest in the fridge.

Roll the pastry out and use to line 10x 9cm fluted the tart tins. Place a generous spoonful of your favourite jam or jams in the centre and bake for 20 minutes.

Remove from the oven and allow to cool for 20 minutes and then turn out.

Tip

You can also do these tarts as little cobblers (see page 36) which require no tins. Pick jams with a high fruit content. Fig is an unusual one to look out for.

Apple and sultana cobbler

Serves 6-8

Filling
2 large Bramley apples,
peeled and thinly sliced
1 large handful sultanas
¼ teaspoon ground
cinnamon
55g soft light brown sugar

This is a very easy recipe to start with. It is meant to look rustic and hand-made, and if you are new to pastry it enables you to feel your way with confidence. A cobbler is traditionally a dish with a rough pastry topping or casing.

For the pastry, see page 55.

Combine all the filling ingredients in a bowl and mix well.

Preheat the oven to 180C/gas mark 4, and line a baking sheet with baking parchment.

Roll the pastry out on a floured surface into a rough circular shape about 5mm thick. Transfer to the lined baking sheet. Pile the filling ingredients in the centre of the pastry and fold the edges in towards the middle. Don't worry if it all looks a bit rough, this is part of the charm of a cobbler. Brush the outside with the lightly whisked egg and dust with caster sugar.

Bake for 40-45 minutes or until brown and golden.

Variation

You can divide the pastry up into 8-10 balls and make individual cobblers. In this case the baking time is likely to be more like 25-30 minutes.

Alternative fruit to use include nectarines, rhubarb, peaches, apricots and figs.

Pecan and maple streusel cheesecake

225g shortbread
35g unsalted butter (less if the shortbread is homemade)
625g cream cheese
225g light golden brown sugar
125ml cream
3 eggs
1 teaspoon natural vanilla extract or 1 vanilla pod (scraped)

Strusel topping
25g butter
50g pecans (roughly chopped)
75g shortbread (crumbled, but still with texture)
25g light golden brown sugar

Maple sauce
35g butter
50g caster sugar
75ml maple syrup
125ml cream

This is a sublime and extremely rich baked cheesecake. Streusel means to scatter or sprinkle.

Grease and line a 23cm spring-form tin. Crush the shortbread (quickest way is between two sheets of greaseproof using a rolling pin). Melt the butter, mix the shortbread up with it and sprinkle over the base. It doesn't need to be as firm as a chilled cheesecake. Don't worry about pressing it into the edges.

Beat the cream cheese and sugar together. Gradually beat in the eggs. Stir in the cream and vanilla extract. Pour over the biscuit base and bake in a pre-heated oven 140C/gas mark 1 for 50 minutes to one hour. It will still have a slight wobble when cooked and it may have cracked. Don't worry, the streusel topping covers a lot.

For the topping use a non-stick frying pan. Melt the butter over a low heat. Add the pecans and cook gently for one to two minutes. Add the crumbled shortbread and sugar and cook for another 2 to 3 minutes stirring frequently. Leave to cool slightly and then pour over the cooled cheesecake. Allow to cool to room temperature.

Put all the sauce ingredients in a saucepan and bring slowly to the boil. Cook until the mixture has become a light caramel colour. This will take about 5 minutes. Serve with the cheesecake.

Serve with whipped cream.

Ultimate chocolate cake

Serves 12

275g unsalted butter
125ml strong coffee
275g dark chocolate
(70% cocoa solids)
110g self-raising flour
110g plain flour
¼ teaspoon bicarbonate
of soda
225g dark brown sugar
225g light brown sugar
30g cocoa powder
100ml buttermilk
4 medium-sized eggs, beaten

Icing

350g dark chocolate
425ml double cream
1.5 tsp light brown sugar
(53% cocoa solids), broken
into pieces

The title says it all, a cake to indulge in. It is very moist and rich, and will keep for up to a week in an airtight container in a cool dry place.

Preheat the oven to 150C/gas mark 2. Have ready a 20 x 10cm loose-bottomed round cake tin lined with baking parchment.

Melt the butter, coffee and chocolate together in a bowl over barely simmering water. Put all the dry ingredients in a large bowl, then add the melted butter and chocolate mix and finally the buttermilk and eggs.

Pour into the lined tin and bake for 1¾ - 2 hours. Remove from the oven and leave to cool on a wire rack.

Melt the chocolate in a bowl over a saucepan of simmering water. Set aside to cool. Combine the cream with the sugar and bring to the boil then let it cool to room temperature before gently combining with the chocolate. Ice the cake with the help of a palette knife.

To assemble, cut the cake in half horizontally. Spread two-thirds of the icing over the bottom half, and cover with the top half of the cake. Spread the remaining icing over the sides first and then over the top.

Cheat's Banoffi

Base

275g digestive biscuits, made into crumbs
125g unsalted butter, melted
30g caster sugar

Filling

250g dulce de leche or condensed milk (see below)
5 bananas, peeled and sliced
250ml cream, whipped
2 Cadbury's Flakes

The 'cheat' is in the toffee (see below). After that this is quite a traditional recipe simply using the best ingredients.

Line a 20cm spring-form tin with baking parchment.

Put the digestive crumbs in a bowl, add the melted butter and caster sugar and mix well. Spread out as evenly as possible over the lined base of the tin. Refrigerate for at least an hour (this will keep for a day or so in the fridge if covered with clingfilm).

Spread the dulce de leche or 'toffeeised' condensed milk over the biscuit base. Top with bananas, and cover with whipped cream and flaked chocolate.

. . . .

If dulce de leche is hard to find, you can simmer a sealed can of condensed milk for three hours, in a saucepan of water. Take care to ensure the water does not boil away. Allow to cool overnight. This will keep like this for a few weeks. When opened, the condensed milk will have miraculously turned to toffee.

Lemon curd cake

225g butter
225g caster sugar
4 eggs
225g self raising flour
(sieved)
1 lemon (rind of one and
juice of half)
1 teaspoon baking powder
(sieved)
(If you like you can decorate
the cake with lemon curd
and glacia icing on top.)

Grease and line a 23cm spring form tin with parchment paper.

Cream the butter and sugar until light and fluffy. Add the eggs gradually (making sure you do not curdle the mixture) with the flour and baking powder, then add the lemon rind and juice. Place in prepared tin and bake at 170C/gas mark 3 for 55 minutes to 1 hour. Remove from the oven and cool on a wire rack.

Lemon butter icing for the sides of the cake

25g butter (softened)
50g icing sugar
zest of 1 lemon
1 tablespoon lemon juice

Place all ingredients in a bowl and beat until light and fluffy.

Glacia icing for the top of the cake

275g icing sugar
1 tsp lemon juice

Mix everything in a bowl.

To decorate the cake cut the top off the cake and whiz in a food processor, then place on a tray in the oven for five minutes to toast. Cut the cake into three horizontally and cover each layer with lemon curd. Cover the side of the cake with the butter icing and roll the cake in the cake crumbs. Cover the top of the cake in Glacia Icing. Decorate with lemon slices.

Lemon Curd

Grated zest and juice of
5-6 lemons
225g unsalted butter, diced
275g sugar
10 eggs, lightly beaten

To make the lemon curd put the lemon zest and juice, butter and caster sugar in a bowl over a saucepan of simmering water, making sure the bowl does not touch the water. Stir occasionally until the butter has melted and the sugar dissolved. Sieve and then stir in the eggs and leave for 40 minutes to one hour, stirring occasionally. The curd is ready when it coats the back of the wooden spoon.

Remove from the heat, leave to cool and then refrigerate.

Chocolate

Melt the chocolate in a bowl sitting in a bowl over barely simmering water. If you overheat chocolate it goes grainy.

Scones

These do not triple in size as some would have you believe. Roll out to the same size as the top of the cutter.

Once you have added milk to your mixture the raising agent has started working. Don't delay in transferring to your preheated oven.

With bread soda you use buttermilk; with baking powder you use fresh milk.

Scones can be prepared to breadcrumb stage and then left overnight for the milk to be added in the morning.

Pastry

All pastry freezes well for up to 3 months, so why not make a double batch.

Cookie dough

Once made up this keeps for up to a week in the fridge.

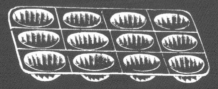

Mars Bar Biscuits

Tin Size: 30cm x 20cm x 4cm
6 x 65g Mars Bars
200g butter
200g Rice Crispies
250g milk chocolate

Cut the butter and Mars Bars into small chunks and place in a saucepan. Put over a low heat and stir with a balloon whisk until melted.

Add the Mars bars/butter mixture to the Rice Crispies in a large bowl. Stir well until all ingredients are combined. Put into a lined tin 30cmx20cmx5cm and press down with the palm of your hand until firm. Melt the chocolate either in a microwave on low for one to two minutes, or over a saucepan of simmering water. Pour over the biscuits, spread evenly with a palate knife and leave to set. When set turn out on a board and cut into squares.

Chocolate and raspberry truffle cake

3 medium-sized eggs
75g caster sugar
25g cornflour
50g cocoa powder

Truffle mixture

225g frozen raspberries,
soaked in 4 tablespoons
crème de cassis
450g dark chocolate (at least
53% cocoa solids), broken
into pieces
600ml double cream, lightly
whipped

Preheat the oven to 170C/gas mark 3. Line a 23cm springform tin with baking parchment.

Whisk the eggs and sugar with an electric whisk until the mixture reaches the ribbon stage, about 10 minutes. Sieve the cornflour and cocoa together and fold into the egg mixture very lightly.

Pour into the lined tin and bake for 15 minutes or until just firm to the touch in the centre.

Remove from the oven and while still warm soak the cake with the juice from the raspberries. Allow the cake to cool totally and then remove from the tin. Re-line the tin with clingfilm and return the cake.

To make the truffle mixture, melt the chocolate in a bowl over barely simmering water, allow to cool slightly, then fold into the cream. Pour half the chocolate mixture over the cake in the lined tin, top with the raspberries and then cover with the remaining chocolate cream.

Place in the fridge for at least 2 hours or until set. Decorate with extra raspberries and even pink rose petals if you like.

Variations

Soak the cake in 4 tablespoons Cointreau mixed with the juice of a half orange and 2 tablespoons orange marmalade. Add the finely grated zest of 2 oranges to the chocolate cream.

Strawberry and mascarpone tart

1 quantity sweet shortcrust
pastry
1 egg for the egg wash
500g mascarpone
25g caster sugar
125ml Greek style yoghurt
250ml cream
1 vanilla pod
zest of 1 orange
500g fresh strawberries,
hulled
3 tablespoons jam –
strawberry or apricot

Pre-heat the oven to 180C/gas mark 4. Roll the pastry out and line a 26cm loose bottomed, fluted tart tin. Bake the pastry blind for 20 minutes (se page 55). Remove the baking beans and brush with egg wash. Bake for a further five minutes.

Combine the sugar, mascarpone, yoghurt and cream. Divide the vanilla pod lengthways and scrape out the centre. Add the seeds to the mascarpone mixture and mix together.

In a saucepan heat the jam with three tablespoons of water. Sieve to remove any pips. Trim the edges of the pastry case by going around with a sharp knife. Do this while it's still in the tin. Spread the mascarpone filling in the case. Arrange the strawberries in a decorative "this only took me minutes to do" kind of way. With a pastry brush glaze the strawberries with the jam mixture.

Brown sugar meringues

36 x 6cm meringues

6 medium-sized egg whites
180g caster sugar
180g soft dark brown sugar

Filling
Three tablespoons Bailey's
Irish Cream, folded into
500ml whipped double
cream.

A slightly different take on an old favourite. The brown sugar gives these meringues a deeper, more rounded flavour. Meringues keep for 4-5 days in an airtight container. Meringues made with caster sugar will keep for a few days longer still, as caster sugar has a low moisture content.

Preheat the oven to 110C/gas mark ¼, and line a couple of baking sheets with baking parchment.

Place the egg whites in the metal bowl of a food mixer, add the caster sugar and whisk continuously for 10-15 minutes at the highest speed until tripled in volume. With the motor still running, add the brown sugar a spoonful at a time for 5 minutes or until it is all incorporated.

Shape into mini (teaspoon) or normal (dessertspoon) meringues or, if you are making a roulade, spread out evenly on your baking sheet using a metal spatula. Bake for an hour or until just coloured. The smaller ones will take about 40 minutes.

To check if your meringues are cooked, try and lift off the baking parchment. They should come away easily if they are done. If not return to the oven for a further 10 minutes and repeat. Allow to cool on a wire rack.

To finish spoon the cream on to the flat surface of one meringue and sandwich with another.

Variations
to add to the egg mixture

Chopped/diced toasted
hazelnuts
Nibbed almonds
The meringue can also be baked as a Swiss roll or roulade log. Spread the mixture into a well-lined Swiss roll tin, and bake as above. You then roll it up round the filling.

Top tips

The secret to making meringues is having a clean bowl. Grease is the worst offender: it means the egg whites will not whisk properly. If possible use a bowl that is stainless steel, and always use a (clean) metal spoon to do any folding in.

Eclairs

Makes about 12 large eclairs or 30 profiteroles

A Seventies treat; sticky, creamy and wonderfully chocolatey. Any guilt is washed with glorious nostalgia.

150ml water
50g unsalted butter, diced
60g plain flour
3 medium-sized eggs, well beaten

Chocolate topping

100g chocolate (70% cocoa solids)
3-4 tablespoons single cream or full-fat milk

Filling

250g whipping cream
1 teaspoon icing sugar

Preheat the oven to 200C/gas mark 6.

Put the water in a saucepan with the butter over a moderate heat. As soon as the butter has melted remove from the heat, pour the flour in and beat with a wooden spoon. The mixture will come together into a smooth paste.

Transfer to a food mixer and allow to cool for 5 minutes. Using the K-beater, add the eggs bit by bit, beating vigorously, so you have a smooth, silky paste.

Line a baking tray with greaseproof paper splashed with a little water (just shake wet hands over it a couple of times). Using a piping bag with a 1cm nozzle, pipe into 8cm lengths – or 3cm blobs for profiteroles – leaving space between to allow them to expand.

Bake for 20-30 minutes (15-20 minutes for profiteroles), or until golden brown. Prick each to let out the steam, cook for a further 3 minutes and then transfer to a wire rack to cool.

For the topping, melt the chocolate in a bowl over simmering water. Remove from the heat and whisk in the cream or milk until shiny and glossy.

For the filling, whip the cream and icing sugar together.

Fill each éclair with the sweetened cream mixture, and top with the chocolate mixture.

....

Tip

Make sure the oven is well heated before you put the mixture in.

Fairy buns

Makes 18 buns or 36 baby buns

These are a favourite for children's parties, but it is well worth making an excess as adults seem to rather enjoy them too.

120g unsalted butter
120g caster sugar
a drop of vanilla extract
3 medium-sized eggs, lightly beaten
150g self-raising flour
½ teaspoon baking powder

Preheat the oven to 200C/gas mark 6. Place 18 bun cases on an oven tray

Cream the butter, sugar and vanilla together until light and fluffy. Gradually start adding the eggs, a bit at a time, alternating with the flour and baking powder which stops the mixture curdling. Finally add the remaining flour.

Spoon the mixture into muffin papers and bake for 12-15 minutes (the large) or 7-9 minutes (the baby buns).

Icing
150g icing sugar
2 tablespoons warm water

Combine the icing sugar with warm water and spread over the cakes.

Variations

Add jumbo sultanas and orange zest to the mixture; or orange zest and chocolate chips; or sultanas, diced dried cranberries and a pinch of cinnamon. For chocolate buns replace 25g of the flour with the same weight of cocoa powder.

Gingerbread

Makes 1 loaf cake

110g unsalted butter
110g golden syrup
110g treacle
225g plain flour
1 teaspoon bicarbonate of
soda
1 teaspoon mixed spice
1 dessertspoon ground
ginger, sieved
60g caster sugar
150ml milk
2 medium-sized eggs, beaten

Ginger syrup

100g caster sugar
100ml water
5cm piece fresh root ginger,
peeled and grated

A good gingerbread is deliciously aromatic. The dark texture and spicy flavour a timeless treat. This cake keeps for a week in an airtight container.

Preheat the oven to 150C/gas mark 2. Grease and line a 900g loaf tin with baking parchment.

Melt the butter, syrup and treacle together in a saucepan over a low heat. Sieve the flour, bicarbonate of soda and spices into a bowl, add the caster sugar and mix well. Add the syrup mixture, milk and eggs and mix.

Pour into the prepared tin and bake for 40 minutes or until cooked.

For the ginger syrup, dissolve the sugar in the water with the ginger over a low heat then boil for 2 minutes.

Remove the cake from the oven and drizzle with the ginger syrup while still hot. Allow to cool and serve.

drizzle with the ginger syrup while still hot

Sweet talking

Sugar used to be seen as an evil ingredient, responsible for obesity. Thankfully we have grown up a little. Still an unrefined sugar is better than a sugar refined to pure white.

Sugar is a seasoning rather than an ingredient, and its role is to bring out the character of other ingredients – think of good pastry. If you use too much sugar, like salt, it can take over. Try substituting honey where appropriate.

Cream

In this dairy-rich nation it is surprisingly difficult to find good cream, by which we mean rich, yellow cream that tastes of something. Most is thin, tasteless and boring. Smaller producers are worth seeking out. Crème fraîche - a slightly tart, cultured cream - is more acceptable than it once was. It generally has good texture and a flavour that is both indulgent, rich and piquant.

Chocolate scones

Makes 20

125g unsalted butter, diced
400g plain flour
1 heaped teaspoon baking
powder
100g drinking chocolate
65g caster sugar, plus a little
extra
2 medium-sized eggs, 1
beaten for egg wash
About 200ml milk

The scones are good by themselves, but you could also cut them in half, and then top with whipped cream and a teaspoon of dulce de leche or Nutella and sprinkle with icing sugar.

Preheat the oven to 170C/gas mark 3.

Rub the butter into the flour, baking powder and drinking chocolate until the mixture resembles fine breadcrumbs. Add the sugar and make a well in the middle. Add 1 egg and the milk, and bring the mixture together to form a ball.

Roll out to a 4-5cm thickness. Cut out using a cutter or knife, egg wash and sprinkle with a little sugar

Bake for 15-20 minutes or until golden brown. Check underneath, the base should look well cooked through.

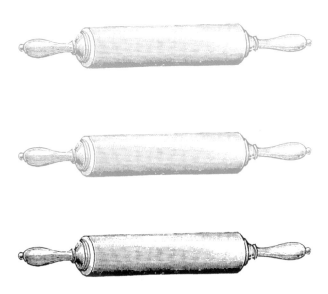

Chocolate orange and cranberry lattice tart

Pastry

225g plain flour
150g unsalted butter, diced
25g caster sugar
2 medium-sized egg yolks
finely grated zest of 1 lemon
about 2 tablespoons water
1 medium-sized egg, beaten

Filling

300g mascarpone cheese
125g ricotta cheese
125g icing sugar
finely grated zest of 3 oranges
2 medium-sized eggs, separated
seeds of 1 vanilla pod
50g dried cranberries, chopped
50g dark chocolate drops (70% cocoa solids)

A particularly stylish tart which incorporates a berry too rarely seen in use outside of its Christmas appearance with turkey. The chocolate and orange partnership is something of a clear winner

Have ready a fluted loose-bottomed 26cm tart tin.

For the pastry, rub the flour and butter together, stir in the caster sugar and make a well in the centre. Add the egg yolks, lemon zest and just enough water to form a ball with the flour mixture. Wrap in clingfilm and leave to rest in the fridge for at least an hour.

Line the tin with two-thirds of the pastry and bake blind (see below). Roll out the remaining third and cut into 14 strips to use for the lattice top.

Preheat the oven to 200C/gas mark 6.

For the filling, beat both cheeses together, then add the sugar, orange zest and egg yolks, and stir until smooth. Whisk the egg whites until firm and fold into the cheese mix. Spread over the cooked pastry base. Sprinkle with the chopped cranberries and chocolate drops.

Lay pastry strips over the top in a lattice style. Brush the pastry strips with the egg wash and bake for 35-40 minutes or until golden brown and set.

Baking blind

Preheat the oven to 190C/gas mark 5. The objective is to dry the pastry out and firm up the shape so nothing leaks. You need to line the interior of your raw pastry base with baking parchment weighted down with baking beans. Bake for between 20 and 30 minutes. Remove the parchment and beans (which can be used again), and egg wash. Return to the oven for 5 minutes. Then continue with the recipe.

Hazelnut and praline mousse cake

Cake
200g shelled hazelnuts
5 medium-sized eggs
150g light brown sugar
150g plain flour
1/2 teaspoon baking powder
35g unsalted butter, melted
and cooled

Praline
225g almonds
vegetable oil for greasing
450g caster sugar
150ml water

Filling 1
1 1/2 sheets gelatine
300ml double cream,
whipped
2 tablespoons very strong
coffee
2 tablespoon Bailey's Irish
Cream

Filling 2
50g dark chocolate (70%
cocoa solids)
300ml double cream,
whipped

To finish
200ml double cream,
whipped

Preheat the oven to 170C/gas mark 3. Grease and line a 25cm springform tin with baking parchment.

Spread the hazelnuts for the cake and almonds for the praline out on separate trays and roast at the top of the oven for 3 minutes. Remove, shake and return to the oven for another 2 minutes. Allow to cool for a few minutes. Blitz the hazelnuts for the cake in a food processor. Scatter the praline almonds on a lightly oiled roasting tray, and set aside.

For the cake, whisk the eggs and sugar together with a balloon whisk until the mixture reaches the ribbon stage (about 8 minutes). Sift the flour and baking powder together, and fold into the egg mix, alternating with the ground hazelnuts and melted butter.

Place in the tin and bake for 30-35 minutes, or until firm to the touch. Cool on a wire rack.

Praline: Combine the sugar with the water in a saucepan. Place on the heat and stir with a wooden spoon until the sugar dissolves. Leave to boil for about 10 minutes. You want the colour of the mixture to be a bit darker than golden syrup. Remove from the heat and pour over the toasted nuts on the tray. Leave to cool completely, and set. Break with a rolling pin or blitz in a food processor for a finer praline. Place on a tray.

Filling 1: place the gelatine and 50ml of the cream in a bowl and leave to sponge. Melt in a microwave until there are no lumps. Add another tablespoon of cream to cool the mixture. Lightly whisk the remaining cream, then add the coffee and Bailey's along with the cooled gelatine mix.

Filling 2: melt the chocolate and fold into the lightly whipped cream.

To assemble the cake, cut the cake in two horizontally. Re-line the springform tin with clingfilm. Place one-half of the cake in the bottom of the tin, and cover with the chocolate cream filling. Put the Bailey's filling on top of that, then replace the top half of the cake. Chill well in the fridge, preferably overnight. Remove the cake from the tin.

Cover the edges in whipped cream, then roll in the praline. Cover the top with whipped cream and sprinkle with the remaining praline.

Baked summer berry cheesecake

Makes 1 23cm cheesecake

Base

300g plain shortbread biscuits
60g unsalted butter, melted

Filling

550g cream cheese
200g caster sugar
juice and finely grated zest of 1 lemon
3 medium-sized eggs
150ml double cream
150g ricotta cheese
225g summer berries

Topping

40ml crème fraîche
3 tablespoons fresh berries

A classic baked cheesecake with the benefit of summer berries; colourful and dare we suggest, good for you!

Covered with clingfilm, this cheesecake will keep in the fridge for 3-4 days.

Preheat the oven to 150C/gas mark 2. Line a 23cm springform tin with baking parchment.

Crush the shortbread biscuits and mix with the melted butter. Spread evenly over the base of the tin.

Mix the cream cheese, sugar, lemon juice and zest in a mixer until smooth. Beat in the eggs one at a time, then pour in the cream and finally add the ricotta.

Spoon into the tin and spread the fruit evenly over the top. Slightly dip the berries into the mixture to stop them burning.

Bake for 50 minutes, when the cake should still have a wobble. Allow to cool in the tin.

To serve, cover the top with crème fraîche

and sprinkle
with
fresh berries.

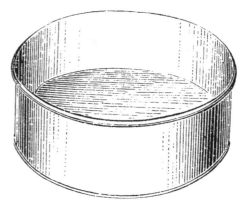

Avoca multi-seed bread

Makes one large loaf

200g plain flour
350g coarse brown flour
50g bran
25g whatgerm
2 heaped teaspoons baking powder
1 level teaspoon salt
1 tablespoon sesame seeds
1 tablespoon poppy seeds
2 tablespoons sunflower seeds
1 tablespoon linseeds
2 tablespoons pumpkin seeds
1 tablespoon treacle
750-800ml milk

Whether for mopping up the oil-infused juices of a tomato salad in summer or eating with a thick slab of juicy ham and cheese in winter this is a great all-round loaf. You can vary the seeds and indeed add fruit. It keeps well for a few days and makes the most delicious toast in the morning.

Mix all the dry ingredients together in a large bowl. Add the treacle and enough milk to make a moist dough, like stiff porridge. Place in a greased 900g baking tin and bake in an oven, preheated to 180C/gas mark 4 for one hour, or until the loaf is well browned and sounds hollow when turned out of the tin and tapped underneath.

Leave

on

a

wire rack

to cool.

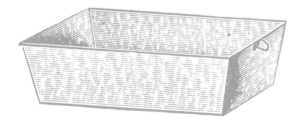

Old-fashioned sandwich sponge cake

5 large eggs
150g caster sugar
150g plain flour, sieved

Filling and topping
raspberry or strawberry jam
200ml whipping cream,
whipped
fresh raspberries or
strawberries, the latter
halved
icing sugar

Old-fashioned certainly, and a key ingredient in any Irish teatime spread. Very easy to do and very light eating, relatively speaking.

Preheat the oven to 170C/gas mark 3. Have ready 2 x 16cm sponge tins, lined with baking parchment.

Beat the eggs and caster sugar together with an electric balloon whisk until the thick ribbon stage is reached. This takes about 10 minutes. Very gently with a metal spoon, fold in the sieved flour.

Spread the mixture evenly between the tins, and bake for 20-25 minutes or until firm to the touch. Remove and cool on a wire rack.

When totally cold top the first cake with jam first, then cream, then berries. Place the second cake on top. Dust with sieved icing sugar and decorate with flowers and strawberries

••

Tip

This cake requires the freshest eggs possible. If you can get them, duck eggs work really well.

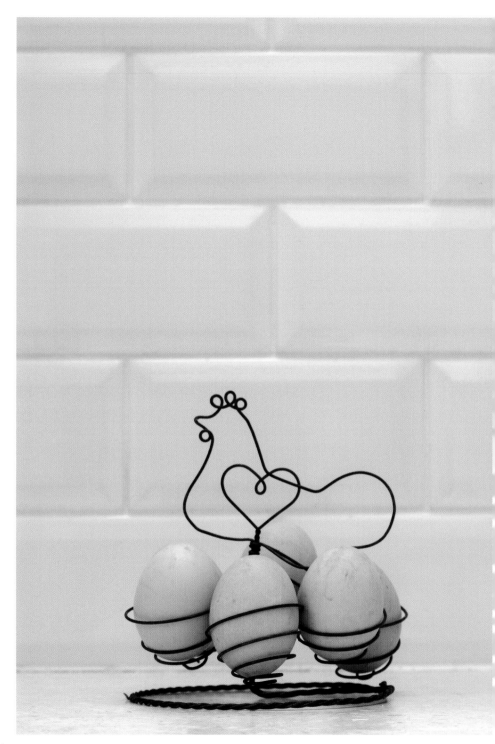

Eggs

Always use organic and free-range eggs. The colour of the yolks is crucial for a good sponge, for example. Duck eggs are surprisingly good for baking.

Fruit

Ripeness is all when it comes to fruit, and this is no less true when it comes to baking. The difference between a pear you want to eat and one you should be cooking with is negligible. Sure, you can add sugar to aid the sweetness, but this is really not the point. If a fruit eats well it will bake well.

How do you tell ripe fruit? Most of it has a gloriously sweet eat-me fragrance, the kind that leaves you in little doubt.

Flour

The flour and butter you use is crucially important. Good butter and flour form the bedrock of so many teatime treats.

Organic flour is preferable, but as with so much in baking it is worth experimenting with brands to find one you like.

Butter

Margarine is not butter and never will be, it just isn't good enough. It is better to use unsalted butter for baking. Again find a brand you like.

f

l

o

u

r

Festive spiced biscuits

Makes about 12 x 8cm biscuits

350g plain flour
2 teaspoons ground ginger
½ teaspoon bicarbonate of soda, sieved
100g butter, diced
175g soft light brown sugar
1 medium-sized egg
4 tablespoons golden syrup

These are good served at teatime, but also make a great end to a meal served with coffee or mint tea. Decorate when cold with icing, silver and gold balls (for an adult version) or with sprinkles, jelly tots or Smarties for children

Preheat the oven to 170C/gas mark 3.

Sift the flour, ginger and soda into a bowl. Rub in the butter until the mixture is like breadcrumbs, then stir in the sugar. Make a well in the centre, add the egg and the syrup, and mix together to form a dough.

Knead the dough lightly on a floured surface, then roll out until 1cm thick. Cut out with 8cm cookie cutters. Place on a greased baking sheet and refrigerate for an hour.

Bake for 15 minutes or until golden brown.

Allow the biscuits to cool slightly, then transfer to a wire rack. They will keep for around 5 days if in an airtight container.

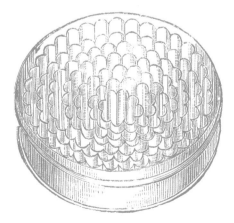

Makes about 25 cookies

300g butter at room temperature
1 egg
375g caster sugar
450g plain flour, sifted
½ teaspoon baking soda
250g chocolate chips or fruit

Making cookies is one of the easist of things to do. Children can join in and you can vary the added ingredients. The secret to good cookies is not to overwork the dough too much or they become tough. Nice and easy does it. Cool hands and a light touch with the mixer are best.

Beat the butter, egg and sugar in a food mixer with the K-beater or paddle attachment until completely combined. Mix in the flour, then the baking soda. Finally add the chocolate chips or fruit.

The dough should stick together. If it is too crumbly, it means the butter was not soft enough, so beat for a little longer. If it still does not combine, add two tablespoons of milk.

Wrap the dough in cling film and chill for one hour. Roll out on a floured board to 5mm thick and cut into rounds with a pastry cutter. Place on a baking sheet lined with parchment paper. Bake in an oven preheated to 170C/gas mark 3 for 20-25 minutes, or until golden brown. Transfer to a wire rack and cool.

Ingredients to add to your cookies in place of chocolate chips
Sultanas
Raisins
Chopped apricots
Chopped mangos
Smarties
Chopped walnuts

Nuts to use
Almonds
Hazelnuts

Spices to use
1 teaspoon ground ginger
1 teaspoon ground cinnamon
2 teaspoons caraway seeds

Bakewell tart

Serves 10-12

A classic jam and almond gem.

1 quantity shortcrust pastry
(see page 36 apple and
sultana cobbler)
4 tablespoons strawberry or
raspberry jam
75g unsalted butter
75g caster sugar
1 medium-sized egg and 1
egg yolk
a drop of natural almond
essence
65g ground almonds
40g plain flour, sifted
40g flaked almonds

Preheat the oven to 180C/gas mark 4. Have ready a well-greased 23cm fluted flan tin.

Roll out the pastry and use it to line the tin. Spread the jam over the pastry base.

Beat the butter and sugar together until light and fluffy, then beat in the egg, egg yolk and almond essence. Fold in the ground almonds and flour. Spread over the jam and scatter over the flaked almonds.

Bake for 35 minutes, until lightly coloured and firm to the touch. You may need to cover loosely with foil for the last 10 minutes to stop the top browning too much. Remove form the oven and allow to cool.

Serve with lots of thick cream.

Carmelised pecan squares

Makes about 24 squares

Base
225g unsalted butter, diced
275g plain flour
110g icing sugar

Topping
200g unsalted butter, melted
175g runny honey
3 tablespoons double cream
60g soft dark brown sugar
400g shelled pecans,
coarsely chopped

Preheat the oven to 150C/gas mark 2. Line a 36 x 26cm Swiss roll tin with lightly greased baking parchment.

For the base, rub the butter into the flour and sugar until the mixture looks like breadcrumbs. Transfer to the lined tin and spread out as evenly as possible. Bake for 25 minutes or until pale golden.

For the topping, mix the melted butter with the honey, cream and brown sugar. Stir in the chopped pecans, spread evenly over the base and bake for a further 15-20 minutes.

Allow to cool before cutting into squares. These will keep in an airtight container for 4-5 days

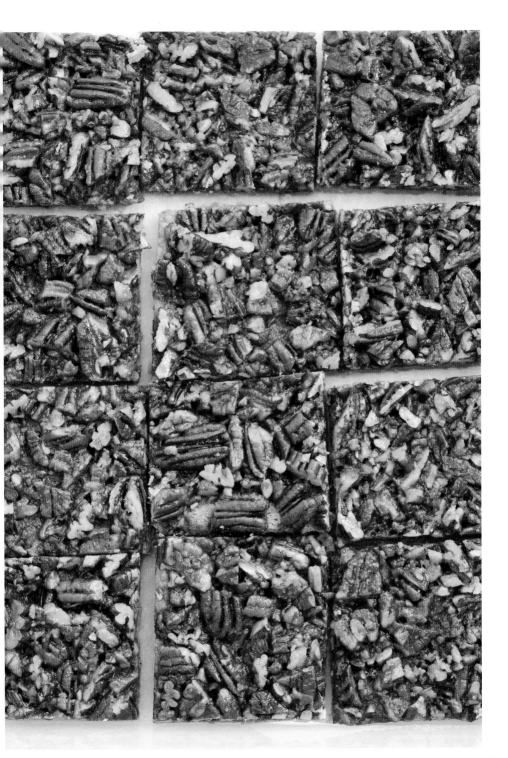

Jumbo sultana and cranberry scones

Makes 8 large or 16 small

125g unsalted butter, diced
400g plain white flour
100g wholewheat flour
1 rounded teaspoon baking
powder
65g demerara sugar, plus
extra for finishing
50g jumbo sultanas
50g dried cranberries
2 large eggs, 1 beaten for
egg wash
approx. 250ml milk

Preheat the oven to 170C/gas mark 3.

Rub the butter into the flours and baking powder until the mixture resembles fine breadcrumbs. Mix in the sugar and fruit, and make a well in the middle. Add 1 egg and the milk, and bring the mixture together to form a ball.

Roll out to a 4-5cm thickness. Cut out using a cutter or knife, brush with the beaten egg wash, and sprinkle with extra brown sugar.

Bake for 15-20 minutes or until golden brown. Check underneath, the base should look well cooked through.

Variations

Add chopped dried dates, apricots, prunes, dried apple or mango to the mixture instead of the sultanas and cranberries

Pear and Almond Scones

Makes 8 large or 16 small

125g unsalted butter, diced
500g plain white flour
1 rounded teaspoon baking
powder
65g caster sugar
2 large pears, peeled, cored
and diced
1 large egg, beaten
225ml milk
3 drops vanilla extract
a handful of flaked almonds

The fruit makes these scones moist in the centre and the subtle vanilla complements the flavours well.

Preheat the oven to 170C/gas mark 3.

Rub the butter into the flour and baking powder until the mixture resembles fine breadcrumbs. Add the sugar and mix well, then stir in the diced pear, egg and milk and vanilla. You need a reasonably dry mixture, so if the pears are very juicy, reduce the milk slightly.

Roll the mixture out to a 4-5cm thickness. Cut out using a cutter or knife and sprinkle over the flaked almonds.

Bake for 15-20 minutes or until golden brown. Check underneath, the base should look well cooked through.

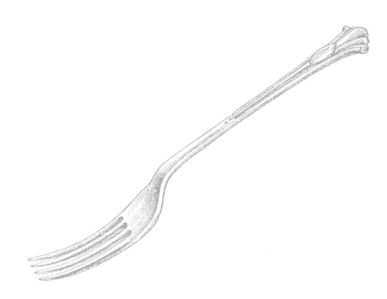

Editor Hugo Arnold
Photography Georgia Glynn Smith
Art Direction and Design Lucy Gowans
Production Tim Chester

Text © 2007 Hugo Arnold
Photography © Georgia Glynn Smith

First published in 2007 by Avoca Ltd,
Kilmacanogue, Co Wicklow
Reprinted in 2008

Printed and bound in Hong Kong by South Sea
International Press

Cataloguing-in-publication datea:
A catalogue record for this book is available
from the British Library
ISBN 978-0-9538152-3-4

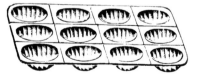